Is it magnetic or nonmagnetic?

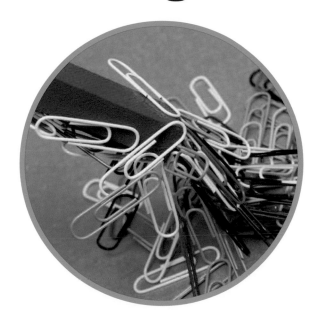

Trudy Rising

Crabtree Publishing Company

www.crabtreebooks.com

Author: Trudy Rising
Publishing plan research and development:
   Sean Charlebois, Reagan Miller
   Crabtree Publishing Company
Project development: Clarity Content Services
Project management: Karen Iversen
Project coordinator: Kathy Middleton
Editors: Trudy Rising, Kathy Middleton
Copy editor: Dimitra Chronopoulos
Proofreader: Reagan Miller
Design: First Image
Photo research: Linda Tanaka
Production coordinator: Margaret Amy Salter
Prepress technician: Margaret Amy Salter
Print coordinator: Katherine Berti

Photographs:
p1 Tommounsey/iStock; p4 left Imaengine/dreamstime.com, clearimages/ shutterstock; p5 top Gianna Stadelmyer/shutterstock, Dja65/shutterstock, Alan49/shutterstock; p6 iStockphoto/ Thinkstock; p7 Tommounsey/iStock; p8 top clockwise iStockphoto/ Thinkstock, Marques/shutterstock, bonchan/ shutterstock; p9 lower left clockwise brulove/shutterstock, PRILL Mediendesign und Fotografie/shutterstock, PRILL Mediendesign und Fotografie/ shutterstock, hvoya/shutterstock, thumb/shutterstock; p10 left Vlad Ivantcov/Dreamstime.com, Hemera/Thinkstock; p11 top right Marcel Mooij/ shutterstock, middle left Jupiter Images/Thinkstock, Romanchuck Dimitry/ shutterstock; p12 Awe Inspiring Images/ shutterstock; p13 Valueline/ Thinkstock, Frankie_8/ shutterstock; p14 top Ukrphoto/Dreamstime.com, Edgaras Kurauskas/ shutterstock; p15 left Elena Schweitzer/shutterstock, iStockphoto/ Thinkstock; p16 Dan Van Den Broeke/Dreamstime.com; p17 left Patricia Hofmeester/shutterstock, iStockphoto/Thinkstock; p18-19 MilanB/shutterstock; p19 grafica/shutterstock; p21 Art Directors & TRIP/All Canada Photos; p22 mack2happy/shutterstock; cover shutterstock

Library and Archives Canada Cataloguing in Publication

Rising, Trudy L.
   Is it magnetic or nonmagnetic? / Trudy Rising.

(What's the matter?)
Includes index.
Issued also in electronic formats.
ISBN 978-0-7787-2050-8 (bound).--ISBN 978-0-7787-2057-7 (pbk.)

   1. Magnetic materials--Juvenile literature. 2. Magnetism--Juvenile literature. 3. Matter--Properties--Juvenile literature.
I. Title. II. Series: What's the matter? (St. Catharines, Ont.)

QC757.5.R57 2012   j620.1'1297   C2012-900299-2

Library of Congress Cataloging-in-Publication Data

Rising, Trudy L.
Is it magnetic or nonmagnetic? / Trudy Rising.
   p. cm. -- (What's the matter?)
Includes index.
ISBN 978-0-7787-2050-8 (reinforced library binding : alk. paper) --
ISBN 978-0-7787-2057-7 (pbk. : alk. paper) -- ISBN 978-1-4271-7948-7
(electronic pdf) -- ISBN 978-1-4271-8063-6 (electronic html)
1. Magnetism--Juvenile literature. 2. Matter--Properties--Juvenile literature.
I. Title.

QC753.7.R57 2012
538'.4--dc23
           2012000123

Crabtree Publishing Company

www.crabtreebooks.com   1-800-387-7650

Printed in Canada/052019/EF20190404

Published in Canada
Crabtree Publishing
616 Welland Ave.
St. Catharines, ON
L2M 5V6

Published in the United States
Crabtree Publishing
PMB 59051
350 Fifth Avenue, 59th Floor
New York, New York 10118

Published in the United Kingdom
Crabtree Publishing
Maritime House
Basin Road North, Hove
BN41 1WR

Published in Australia
Crabtree Publishing
Unit 3 – 5
Currumbin Court
Capalaba QLD 4157

What is in this book?

What is matter?

Look around you. Everything that you see is made of **matter**. Matter is anything that takes up space and has **mass**. Mass is the amount of material in an object.

You are made of matter.
This book is made of matter, too.

What is a property?

There are different kinds of matter. Every kind of matter has its own **properties**.

Properties describe how something looks, feels, tastes, smells, or sounds. Properties can also tell us how something acts.

Some matter is **magnetic**.

Materials that have a magnetic property can pull, or **attract**, objects with **iron** in them.

Iron is a kind of matter. It is found in many metal objects.

magnet →

iron
pieces

What is attracted?

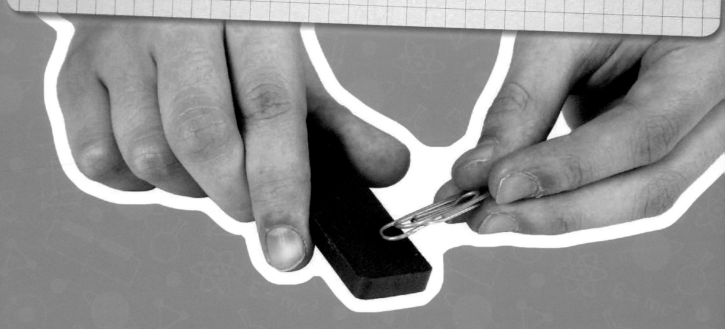

What kind of objects are
attracted to a magnet?

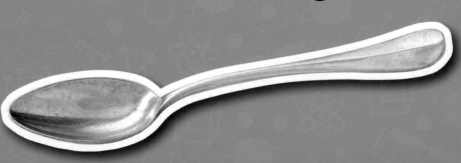

To find out, hold a magnet close to different objects, like the ones shown on these pages.

How can you tell when the object is attracted to the magnet?

What kind of matter is in the objects that are attracted to the magnet?

Many shapes of magnets

Magnets can have different shapes.

A bar magnet has a rectangle shape. A ring magnet has a round shape.

bar magnet ⟶

⟵ ring magnets

A horseshoe magnet is shaped like the letter "U." Some magnets are even shaped like balls.

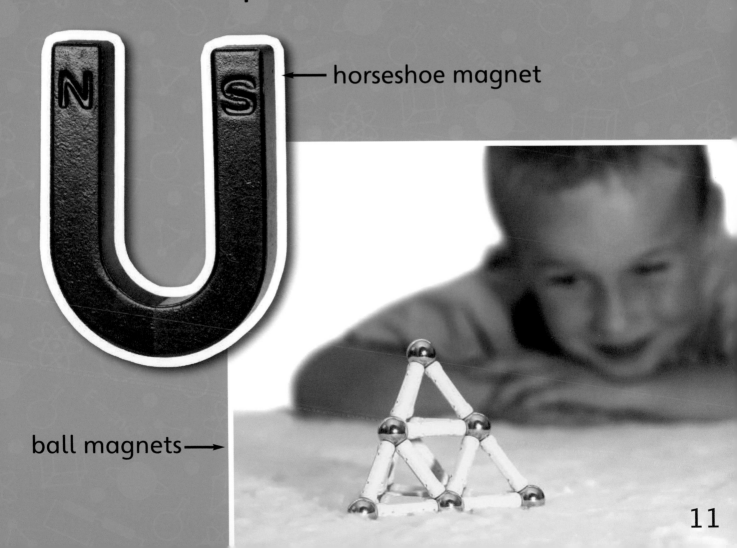

horseshoe magnet

ball magnets

How strong is it?

Some magnets have a stronger attraction to iron than other magnets do.

Try hanging a paper clip from the end of a magnet. Then keep adding paper clips to each other until the chain falls off the magnet.

Some magnets have a strong attraction to iron. Others are weaker. Try some magnets to see which one has the strongest attraction.

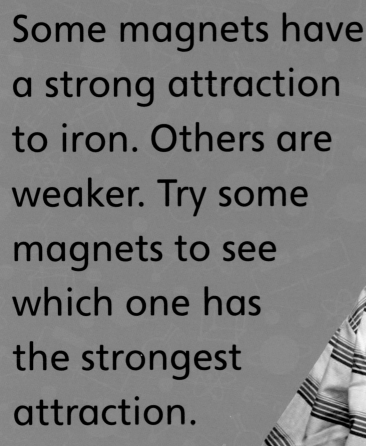

How many paper clips did your magnets attract and hold?

Useful magnets

In some kitchens, cooking tools are held in place by magnets.

Some games have pieces that are magnets.

A magnet on a can opener holds the lid of the can while it is being opened.

? Where else can you find magnets in your home?

Magnets outdoors

In a scrapyard, a huge magnet is used to pick up and sort metal objects.

The magnet is attracted only to objects with iron in them. Other objects stay on the ground.

Machines called metal detectors use magnets to find metal objects, such as coins made with iron, that may be hidden. This person has found a lost ring with a metal detector.

What are poles?

A magnet has two ends. Each end is called a pole. One end of a magnet is called its **north pole**. The other end is called its **south pole**.

The poles on a ring magnet are on the top and bottom sides.

A magnet's strength is strongest at its poles.

Most magnets are marked with the letter "N" to show the north pole. The letter "S" is used to show the south pole.

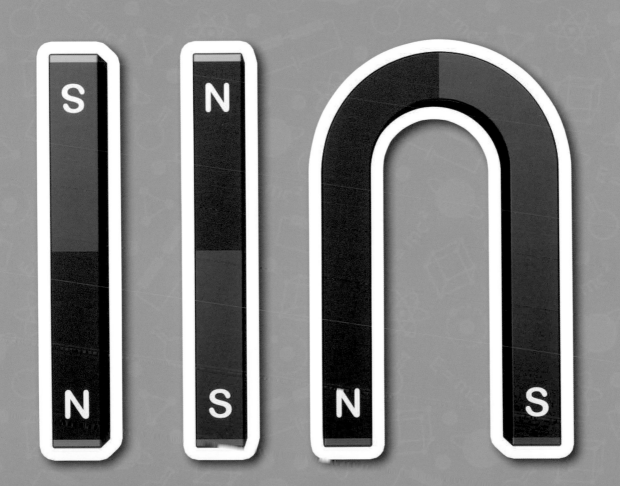

Pushing and pulling

Poles that are different attract each other. The north pole of one magnet will pull toward the south pole of another magnet.

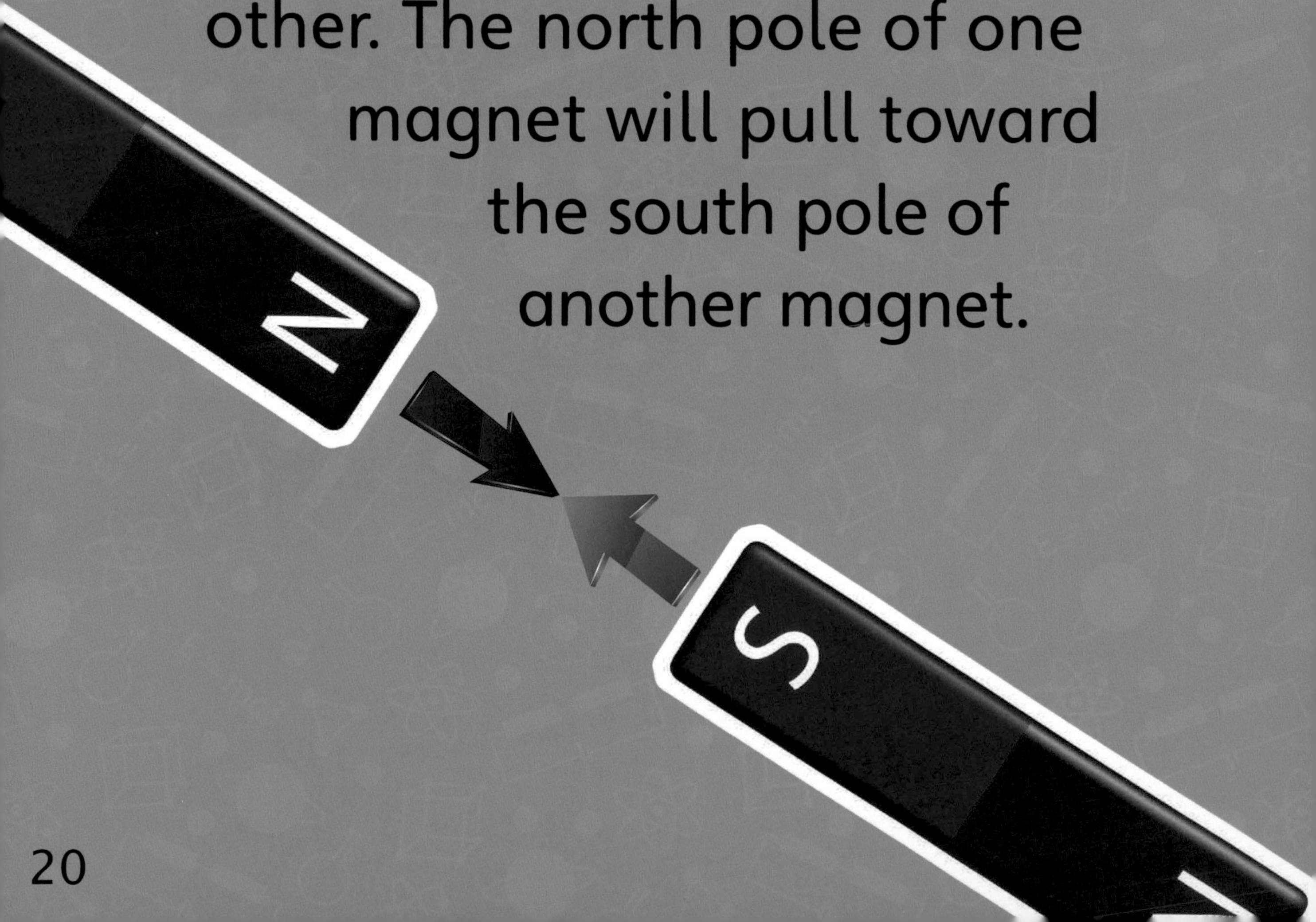

N

S

Poles that are the same **repel**, or push away from, each other. The north pole of one magnet will repel the north pole of another magnet.

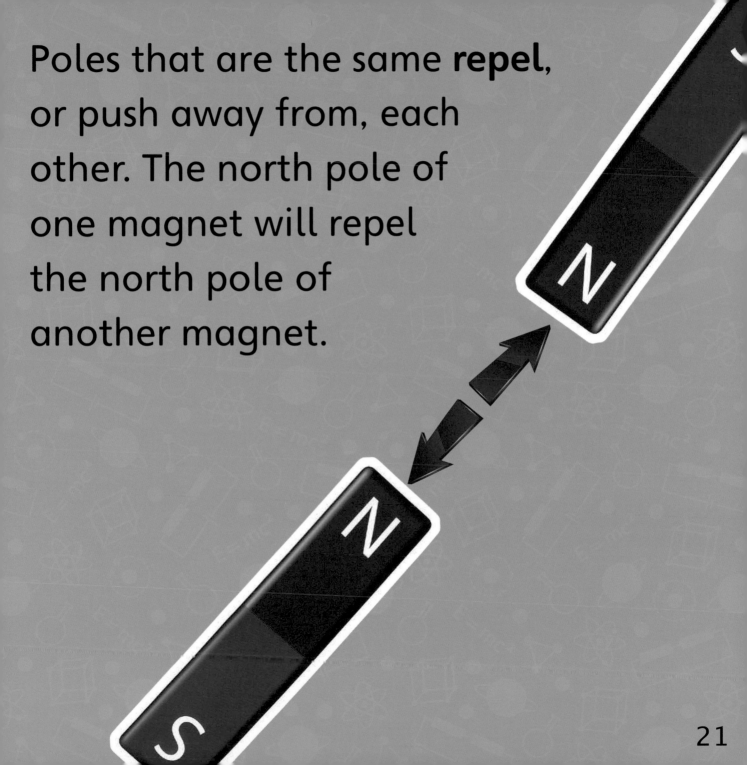

Finding the poles

Imagine you had two magnets. The north and south poles are marked only on magnet #1.

How can you find out which end of magnet #2 is its north pole and which end is its south pole?

Answer: Use magnet #1 to test both ends of magnet #2. The north pole of magnet #1 will attract the south pole of magnet #2.

Words to know and Index

Notes for adults

Objectives
- to introduce children to matter and to the magnetic property of matter
- to classify materials as magnetic or nonmagnetic
- to build observation and inquiry skills

Prerequisite
Because magnetism is a more advanced concept, it would be helpful for children to read other books in the series, such as *Is it flexible or rigid?*, *Is it hot or cold?*, and *Is it smooth or rough?* before reading this book. This will provide children with a working knowledge of other properties and support their understanding of magnetic and nonmagnetic matter.

Questions before reading *Is it magnetic or nonmagnetic?*
"Have you ever played with magnets? What did you find out about them?"

"What is your favorite thing to do with magnets?"

"Have you ever seen a magnet used outside your home or school? Tell us about it."

Discussion
Show the children some of your own magnets. Tell them how you use magnets. Read the book to the children or share the reading with them. Encourage the children to use new words they have learned such as "attract" and "repel." Invite the children to use their hands to show what happens when magnets repel each other. Do some "magic" with magnets. Put a paper clip in a glass of water. Ask the children how you could get the paper clip out without getting your hand wet. Use a magnet to do this. Introduce the fact that Earth is a huge magnet. Ask the children if they have ever used a compass and have them tell you how they used it. Please note that cobalt and nickel are also magnetic but are not common so are not included in the book.

Extension
Help children make a game that involves magnets for others to play. Suggest that they design one of the following on a piece of thin cardboard: a maze through a forest that a lost squirrel has to follow to get to its home tree, a winding road that a small car has to follow to reach a gas station, or a river that a fish has to swim through to get to the ocean. The children will enjoy coloring the cardboard and then having others use a magnet under the cardboard to guide their small metal squirrel, car, or fish on its journey.